HI-TECH HEALTH CARE

BIONICS IN HEALTH CARE

by Cecilia Pinto McCarthy

BrightPoint Press

San Diego, CA

© 2022 BrightPoint Press
an imprint of ReferencePoint Press, Inc.
Printed in the United States

For more information, contact:
BrightPoint Press
PO Box 27779
San Diego, CA 92198
www.BrightPointPress.com

ALL RIGHTS RESERVED.

No part of this work covered by the copyright hereon may be reproduced or used in any form or by any means—graphic, electronic, or mechanical, including photocopying, recording, taping, web distribution, or information storage retrieval systems—without the written permission of the publisher.

LIBRARY OF CONGRESS CATALOGING-IN-PUBLICATION DATA

Names: McCarthy, Cecilia Pinto, author.
Title: Bionics in health care / by Cecilia Pinto McCarthy.
Description: San Diego : BrightPoint Press, 2022. | Series: Hi-tech health care | Includes bibliographical references and index. | Audience: Grades 7-9
Identifiers: LCCN 2021009969 (print) | LCCN 2021009970 (eBook) | ISBN 9781678201845 (hardcover) | ISBN 9781678201852 (eBook)
Subjects: LCSH: Artificial organs--Juvenile literature. | Prosthesis--Juvenile literature. | Bionics--Juvenile literature. | Medical innovations--Juvenile literature.
Classification: LCC RD130 .M43 2022 (print) | LCC RD130 (eBook) | DDC 617.9/5--dc23
LC record available at https://lccn.loc.gov/2021009969
LC eBook record available at https://lccn.loc.gov/2021009970

CONTENTS

AT A GLANCE	**4**
INTRODUCTION A NEW ARM	**6**
CHAPTER ONE WHAT IS THE HISTORY OF BIONICS IN HEALTH CARE?	**14**
CHAPTER TWO HOW DO BIONICS IN HEALTH CARE WORK?	**28**
CHAPTER THREE HOW ARE DOCTORS USING BIONICS TODAY?	**40**
CHAPTER FOUR WHAT'S NEXT FOR BIONICS IN HEALTH CARE?	**56**
Glossary	74
Source Notes	75
For Further Research	76
Index	78
Image Credits	79
About the Author	80

AT A GLANCE

- Bionics in health care are used to replace missing body parts or fix parts that do not function properly. Medical bionics combine biology, medicine, and engineering.

- A prosthesis is an artificial device that replaces a body part such as a leg or an eye. Some prostheses are bionic. Bionic parts are electronically or mechanically powered.

- Humans have been replacing body parts for centuries. Some ancient prosthetic body parts include eyes, teeth, feet, and legs.

- Wartime amputations increased the need to improve prosthetic limb technology.

- A bionic prosthesis works by receiving and interpreting electrical signals from the body. The signals tell the prosthesis how to move.

- Bionic limbs can sometimes be bulky and uncomfortable. Engineers have found ways to create new bionics that are both comfortable and secure.

- Most of today's bionic limbs can be easily put on and removed as needed.

- Modern bionic body parts include 3D printed limbs, bionic eyes, and bionic ears.

- Medical bionics of the future may include brain-controlled prosthetics and bionic organs. Bionic exoskeletons may be useful for both patients with paralysis and workers in industrial fields.

INTRODUCTION

A NEW ARM

Eleven-year-old Colin loves riding his bike. But steering is an exhausting challenge. Like millions of people around the world, Colin is missing part of an arm. He was born without a right forearm and hand. Colin has worn several types of artificial arms. But none have been comfortable. Most were heavy and awkward to use. One just had a hook for a hand. Worst of

Artificial arms can improve the lives of the people who need them.

all, Colin is embarrassed by his fake arm.

People stare. And kids at school sometimes

make unkind comments.

A new type of artificial arm has changed Colin's life. The arm was made just for him. Engineers took a computer scan of Colin's right upper arm. They used the scan to design an artificial arm to fit his natural limb. Colin's new arm is lightweight. The hand has fingers and a thumb with moveable joints. Now Colin can grab onto and turn his bike's handlebars. The new limb does not pop out. It stays comfortably in place. Colin's favorite thing about his new arm is the Iron Man cover that snaps over it. Everyone thinks it's awesome. It makes

Prosthetic limbs help make everyday activities possible.

Colin feel cool and confident, just like his favorite superhero.

REPLACING BODY PARTS

Colin's artificial arm is a type of **prosthesis**. A prosthesis is an artificial device that replaces a body part such as an arm, leg, or eye. Some prostheses are bionic. Bionic parts are electronically or mechanically powered. They replace missing body parts or fix body parts that do not work properly.

Medical bionics combine biology, medicine, and engineering. To develop bionic body parts, scientists work alongside medical professionals. They study how the

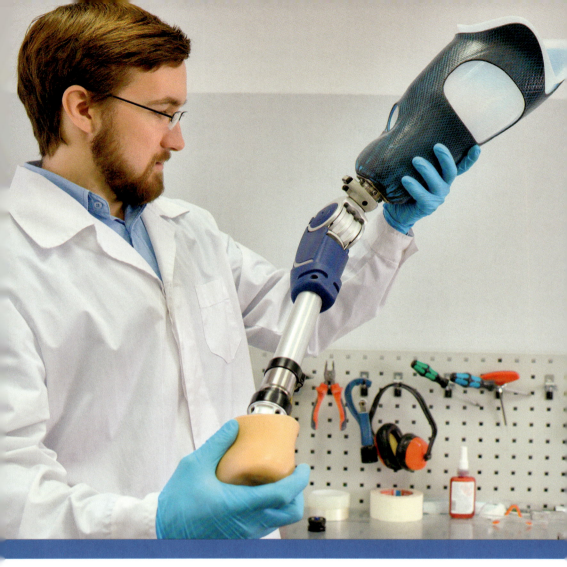

Engineers making prostheses must have a good understanding of how the body works.

body part functions. They learn how the part works with other body systems. With this information, scientists build bionics

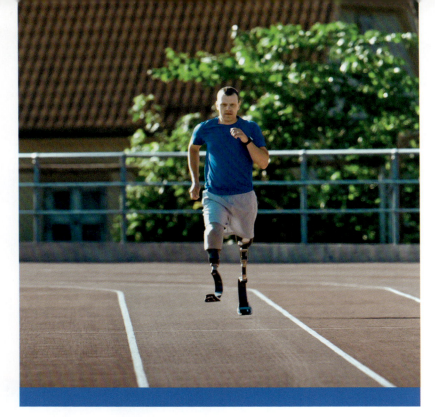

People can participate in athletic activities using carbon fiber prosthetics.

that **mimic** real body parts. Bionic parts improve people's lives. For example, with a bionic ear, a deaf child can hear her mother's voice for the first time.

Patrick Kane contracted a serious infection when he was an infant. Doctors had to remove his right leg below the knee. Through the years, Kane has benefited from bionic technology: "As time has passed and technology has advanced, so too have my limbs. . . . Prostheses have become lighter, faster, and more efficient." Kane explains, "As a child I wore a stiff artificial leg attached with straps that frequently fell off; earlier this summer, I took delivery of a new dynamic right leg with shock absorption and carbon fiber blades."[1]

CHAPTER ONE

WHAT IS THE HISTORY OF BIONICS IN HEALTH CARE?

Humans have been replacing body parts for centuries. Eyes, limbs, and teeth were fashioned from gold, ivory, wood, leather, and glass. Ancient Egyptians and Romans made false eyes from painted clay. The eyes were attached to cloth and

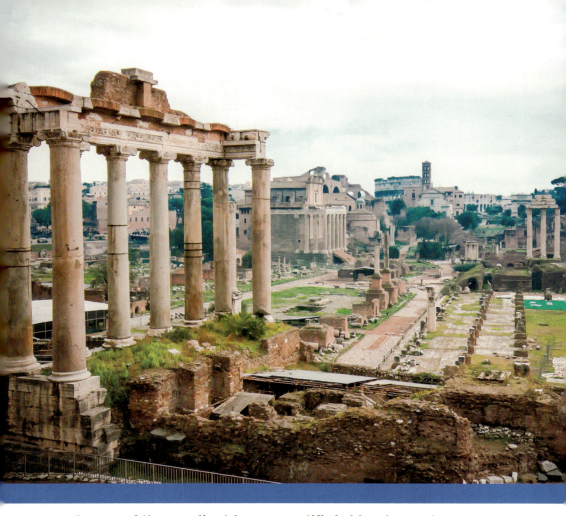

Some of the earliest known artificial body parts date back to ancient Rome.

worn outside of the eye socket. One of the earliest prosthetics ever found is a toe from ancient Egypt. The toe dates to before 600 BCE. It was made from paper soaked in animal glue. It is shaped like a right big toe and part of a foot. The toe has sets of holes on its sides. Laces were woven through the holes to attach the toe to the foot or a sandal.

Another ancient prosthetic is a leg found in Capua, Italy. Dated to 300 BCE, the leg is made of a wooden core wrapped in bronze. It is hollow near the top where the person's padded stump fit in. The wearer probably used a metal waistband and leather straps to attach the leg to his body. Researchers have also unearthed artificial feet at European burial sites. These date

A copy of the Capua leg can be seen in a museum in London, England.

from around the 400s to 700s CE. One foot was a leather pouch stuffed with hay or moss. Another foot was made of wood and bronze. It was attached to a piece of wood that reached to the person's knee.

MOVEABLE LIMBS

Between 1500 and 1900, people built prosthetic limbs with various types of materials. They often used wood, metal, and leather. Gears, springs, and cables made the limbs moveable.

During the 1500s, French surgeon Ambroise Paré designed moveable limbs for soldiers. His mechanical limbs mimicked the movements of real limbs. He built legs with knees that could lock and bend. The arms he designed used pulleys to bend at the elbow. Perhaps his most celebrated design was a mechanical hand. Springs and levers

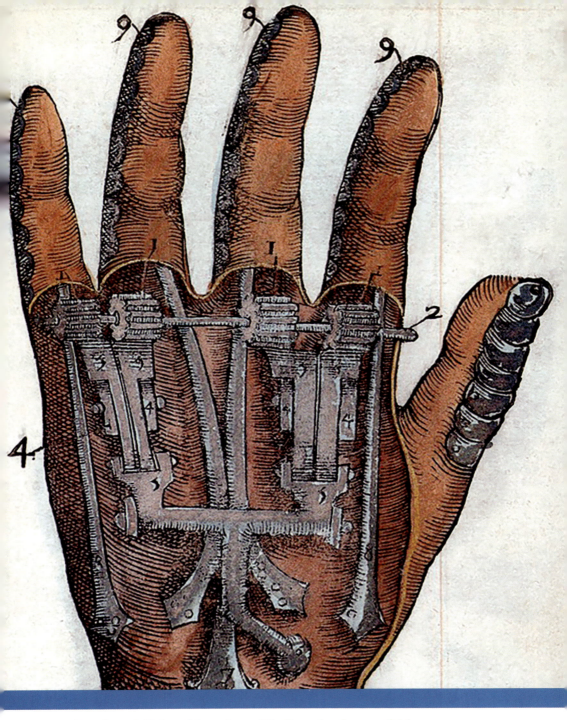

Paré published books with the designs of his artificial body parts.

allowed the fingers to open and close. The user had to operate it with his or her other hand. Still, the moveable limbs were a welcome improvement.

Knights who lost limbs in battle often received realistic-looking metal replacements. German knight Götz von Berlichingen lost his hand in 1505. A skilled artisan made him an iron hand. It had fingers and a thumb with joints. Götz attached the heavy prosthesis to his armor with leather straps. It let him hold his horse's reins and grasp a sword.

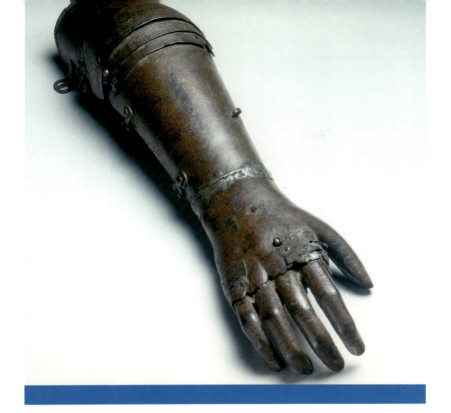

This iron arm is believed to have been owned by Götz von Berlichingen.

MODERN WARFARE

War injuries continued to drive the improvement of prosthetic limbs. During the American Civil War (1861–1865), three-quarters of all surgeries were limb amputations. The amputations fueled the need for better artificial limbs. Inventors thought more about comfort and durability. New legs were cushioned. They were made with steel and rubber.

After World War II (1939–1945) the US government started funding new research. Scientists, surgeons, and engineers studied how limbs function. Modern materials such as plastics and aluminum replaced wood and leather. Artificial limbs included sockets that allowed better motion. Glass eyes were replaced with acrylic versions.

Major wars led to a need for more and better prosthetic limbs. Workers build these limbs in this drawing from 1916.

BIONICS BEGINS

During the mid- to late 1900s, many people experimented with electric prosthetics. Electrically powered prosthetics are myoelectric. That means they are powered by the electrical signals generated by muscles. When a person thinks about moving their artificial limb, muscles in the body send out electric signals. The electric signals travel to the prosthesis. Sensors detect the signals. The prosthesis uses motors to turn those signals into movement.

Bionic body parts have come a long way since the first wooden toes. Today's bionics are complex devices that rely on sensors, computers, and robotic parts. Prosthetics made of plastics and carbon fiber are lightweight and strong. Many modern devices are **implanted** in the body. They work with muscle, bone, and nerves.

LIMB LOSS

The main causes of limb loss are trauma, cancer, and diseases such as diabetes and artery disease. There are approximately 2 million limb amputees in the United States. In the United States, 185,000 amputations are performed each year.

Myoelectric prosthetics represented a big leap forward in bionic technology.

They are powered by signals from the body and brain.

People's ideas about limb loss and bionic body parts have evolved, too. Boston doctor David Crandell has worked with people who have had limbs amputated. He says, "The biggest change I've seen . . . is the societal understanding that losing a limb is not the end. . . . People accept that technology can be part of the solution."[2]

A BIONIC TAIL

Winter is an Atlantic bottlenose dolphin. She lives at the Clearwater Marine Aquarium in Florida. When she was just two months old, Winter was found tangled in a crab trap line. Her tail was badly injured, and part of it had to be removed. After surgery, Winter could not swim properly. Scientists fitted her with a bionic tail that helps her swim. The movie *Dolphin Tale* tells Winter's inspiring story.

CHAPTER TWO

HOW DO BIONICS IN HEALTH CARE WORK?

B ionic body parts are all about making connections to the existing body. This involves the body's electrical signals. "We don't think of the human body as an electrical grid, but it runs off electrical impulses," says bionic eye inventor

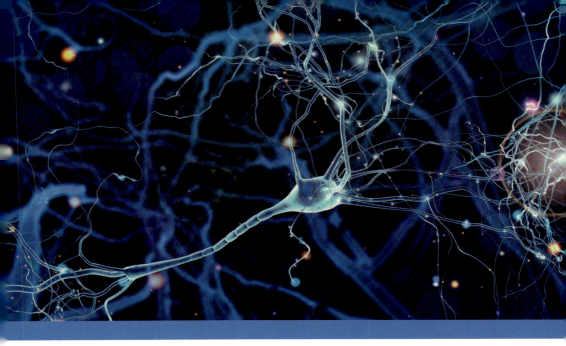

Electrical impulses through the nervous system make the body function. Bionics work alongside this natural process.

Dr. Mark S. Humayun.[3] All bionic body parts must work together with a person's body. They receive information from the body in the form of electrical impulses. The bionic part processes the signals. The part then functions in the proper way based on the signals.

BIONIC LIMBS

Limb prostheses share basic parts. Each limb is constructed around an internal structure called the pylon. Modern pylons are made from carbon fiber. A cover in the shape of an arm or leg goes over the pylon. Bionic limbs may also include parts such as

LIMB COVERS

Ottobock is a company that makes prosthetic limbs. Its silicone leg covers are lifelike. They match a person's skin tone. They even have hair and natural-looking toenails. Many people opt for decorative covers to express their personality. These covers feature designs from movies and comic books such as *Star Wars*, *Frozen*, and *Iron Man*.

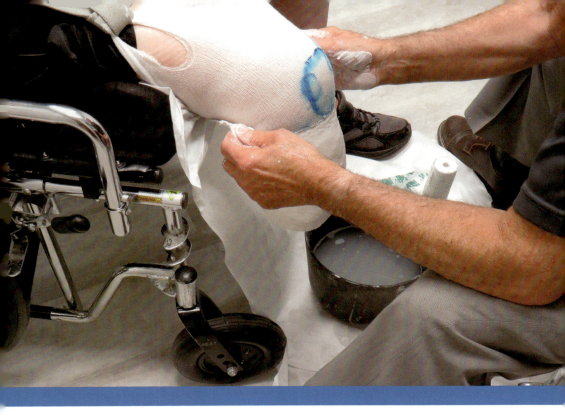

Carefully designing the point where the body connects to the prosthetic is important for the person's comfort.

hands and feet. They may have joints such as elbows, knees, and hips.

The remaining part of the person's limb fits into a plastic holder called the socket. The socket is the link between the body and the prosthetic device. It must be precisely fitted to prevent damaging the skin and tissue. A gel cushion or sock goes over the stump to protect it.

The artificial limb attaches to the body with a suspension system. The simplest systems are belts and straps that hold the prosthesis in place. A common system uses a vacuum that pumps air out of the socket. This creates suction that holds the limb tight as the person moves. Some systems use a pin that locks into the socket. The person presses a button to release the prosthesis. Most of today's bionic limbs are known as "plug and play." This means users can put on and remove their prostheses as needed.

MOVING MUSCLES

Body parts move when muscles contract and relax. Electrical signals from the brain control muscles. When a person wants to move a limb, the brain sends an electrical

PROSTHETISTS

Prosthetists are health care professionals. They create and fit prosthetic limbs. Prosthetists test the strength of the person's remaining limb. They examine how much the person can move his or her limb and joints. They measure a patient's remaining limb to ensure that the bionic limb will fit properly.

The signals that tell limbs to move originate in the brain.

signal to nerve cells in the spinal cord. From there, the signal travels to the muscle along a long nerve fiber called an **axon**. The signal causes muscle fibers to contract. The limb moves.

Bionic body parts must communicate with a person's brain. They do this at

the point where they touch the body.
Prosthetics are controlled by electrical
signals in a person's muscles. Sensors in
the bionic limb attach to electrodes on the
skin. These electrodes are located above
muscles. In some cases, the electrodes are

PHANTOM LIMB SYNDROME (PLS)

After a limb is removed, amputees often feel as though the limb is still attached. The sensations can be nonpainful or painful. Amputees may experience pressure, temperature, itching, stabbing pain, and cramps. This is called phantom limb syndrome (PLS). Doctors do not know for sure what causes PLS. For some, PLS goes away after a few months. People with long-term PLS can be treated with medicines or surgery.

implanted in the muscle. The electrodes pick up signals that the brain sends to the muscles. They also send signals back to the brain.

BIONICS IN ACTION

A woman slips her bionic arm onto her **residual** arm just below the elbow. She wants to reach out and grasp a book from a table. When she thinks about moving her arm and hand, her brain sends a signal to her residual arm muscles. The signal tells the muscles to contract. The sensors in her bionic arm pick up this signal. A controller in the bionic arm translates the signal

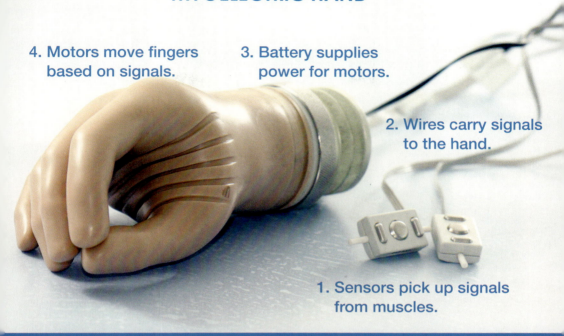

MYOELECTRIC HAND

4. Motors move fingers based on signals.

3. Battery supplies power for motors.

2. Wires carry signals to the hand.

1. Sensors pick up signals from muscles.

Each time a person uses a myoelectric hand, several steps happen in rapid sequence.

into commands. The commands control battery-powered electric motors. They move the limb. Her bionic arm reaches forward and grasps the book.

Joel Gerber, who lost his right hand in an accident, described using a myoelectric

37

Myoelectric prosthetics can give people enough control for many everyday tasks.

prosthesis. "To open the hand, I have to push my muscles up and to close it, I have to push my muscles down. I had to learn how to do that, but now I just do it naturally," he says.[4]

Some bionic limbs have features that give a user more control. The bionic Hero Arm has a button on the back of the hand. Users press it to control the grip. This lets them gently pick up delicate objects such as eggs without crushing them.

Other bionic body parts work in a similar way. They have sensors that send information to the brain. The brain processes the information. It then sends signals back to the bionic part, and the part responds. It takes practice to learn to use bionic limbs.

CHAPTER THREE

HOW ARE DOCTORS USING BIONICS TODAY?

Bionics in health care are evolving quickly. Research is thriving. Scientists are using new materials and technologies. They are building stronger, lighter prosthetics that move more naturally than ever before. These devices are often designed to fit a particular user's body.

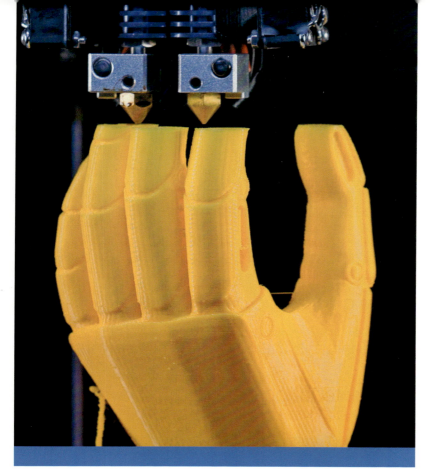

3D printers work by building objects layer by layer.

3D PRINTED BIONIC LIMBS

3D printing technology has revolutionized bionic parts. 3D printers create objects one layer at a time. They use materials such as plastic or nylon. 3D printing allows engineers to create customized body parts. The process starts with a scan of the person's residual limb. Using the scan, doctors can use computer software to design a bionic part that fits perfectly. The design is then sent to a 3D printer. The printer deposits layer after layer of the building material until the prosthetic limb is complete.

Before 3D printing, it could take months for a person to receive a bionic limb. 3D printing makes it possible to make bionic limbs in less than a week. The company Open Bionics makes its customized bionic

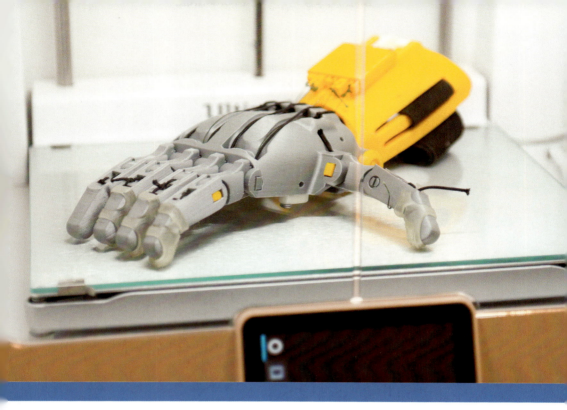

3D printers can be used to make complicated objects, including bionic body parts.

Hero Arm in approximately 40 hours. 3D printing materials are strong and lightweight. Hero Arms are printed from a tough form of nylon. A finished arm weighs less than 2.2 pounds (1 kg). 3D printed limbs are also cheaper to produce.

Other bionic arms can cost up to $95,000.

Hero Arms start at about $3,000.

CONNECTING BONES AND BIONICS

Some bionic limbs can be bulky and

uncomfortable. People may struggle with

PRINTING HEARTS

One benefit of 3D printing is that the process can print soft materials. This is important for creating bionic organs. Bionic hearts made from metal and hard plastic are difficult to install inside the body. That's because they can damage soft tissues. Swiss researchers were able to 3D print a silicone heart. It was the same size as a real human heart. In tests, the heart worked for only about 3,000 beats. Researchers continued to work on making a heart that lasts longer.

getting them on or off. Worst of all, the pressure placed on the residual limb can cause pain. Heat, sweat, and rubbing in the socket cause blisters and sores. People with shorter residual limbs often have trouble controlling their bionic arm or leg.

Doctors have found ways to improve these issues. One surgical method attaches the bionic limb directly to the bone of the residual limb. First, a surgeon inserts a titanium rod into the bone. Over the next few months, bone cells grow over the rod. During a second surgery, a screw is added to the rod. It extends out from the limb.

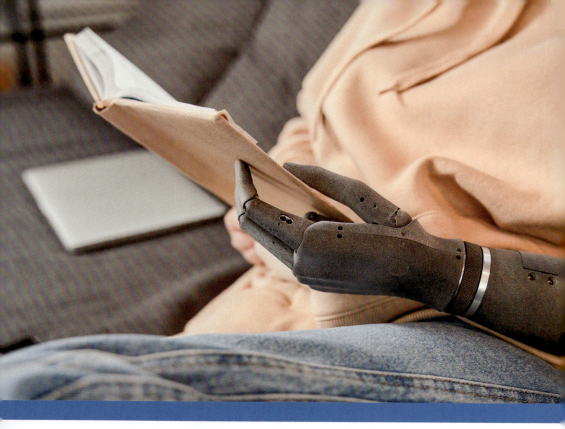

Comfortable bionics can make everyday activities easier.

The bionic limb attaches to this screw.

Combining bone and bionics can improve the lives of people who wear bionic limbs. It eliminates rubbing and skin problems. The limb feels more like it is a part of the person's body. People report that the bionic limb feels more natural. An attached prosthesis is also easier to move.

Johnny Matheny had a rod implanted in his arm bone. He could then attach his bionic limb directly to his body. Matheny says, "Before, the only way I could put the prosthetic on was by this harness with

REROUTING NERVES

People with bionic arms attached to bones often have surgery to reroute their nerves. Surgeons connect the nerves from the remaining arm to muscles nearby, often in the chest. When the person thinks of moving the bionic arm, the chest muscles contract. This creates signals that control the bionic arm. The surgery gives amputees greater control over their bionic arms.

suction and straps; but now . . . the implant does away with all that. It's all natural now. . . . Before, I had limited range; I couldn't reach over my head and behind my back. Now, boom, that limitation is gone."[5]

BIONIC EYES

Prosthetic eyes were once just **cosmetic**. Glass eyes filled up the eye socket. But they did not help a person see. Modern bionic eyes work with the existing eye parts and brain. Unfortunately, they do not fully restore normal sight.

The Argus II is a bionic eye known as a retinal implant. The retina is a layer

Some artificial eyes are used only for appearance. Doctors are working on bionic eyes that can see.

of light-sensitive cells. These cells line the inside of the back of the eye. Light enters the eye and hits the retina. The retina's cells convert the light into electrical signals. Then the signals travel to the brain through the optic nerve. The brain processes the signals into what the person sees.

Some eye diseases destroy the retina. That's where the Argus II can help. It contains an array of sixty electrodes. The array is implanted in the eye and does the work of the damaged retina. The user wears a special pair of glasses. They also wear a processing unit attached to a belt. A small video camera on the glasses takes in images. The images travel to the processing unit, where they are turned into electrical signals. An antenna on the glasses sends the signals to a receiver in the person's eye. The electrodes send these signals to the brain. The brain processes the images into

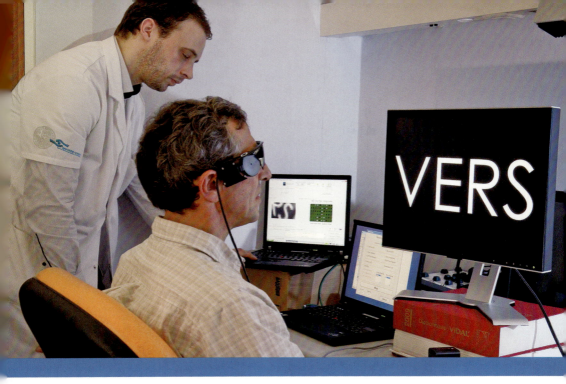

A patient tests the Argus II bionic eye in a laboratory.

light patterns. People with this bionic eye can see flashes of light and dark shapes. They can also sense movement.

BIONIC EARS

Deafness results when the connection between the cochlea and auditory nerve

Part of the cochlear implant device is located outside the head.

is destroyed. The cochlea is a fluid-filled structure in the inner ear. Sound vibrations enter the ear and travel to the cochlea. Tiny hairs inside the cochlea translate the vibrations into electrical signals.

The auditory nerve carries the signals

to the brain. There, they are processed

into sounds.

Bionic ears are also called cochlear

implants. These devices form a connection

that bypasses the cochlea and takes sound

to the auditory nerve. A sound processor

containing a microphone sits behind

the ear. This unit picks up sounds and

sends them to an implanted headpiece.

From the headpiece, the signal travels to

electrodes implanted in the inner ear. The

auditory nerve picks up the signal from

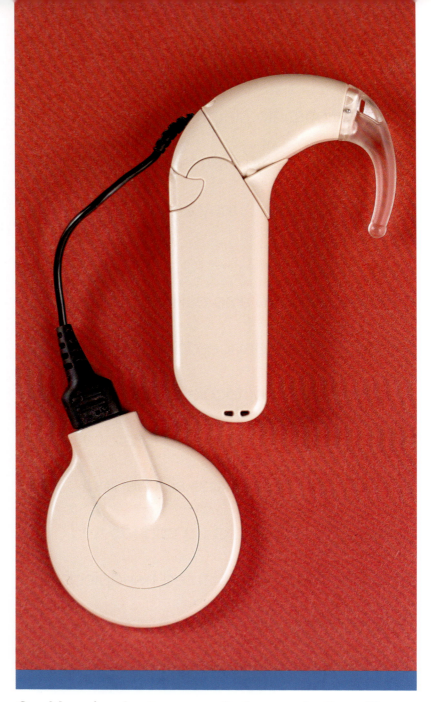

Cochlear implants generally have a battery life of between ten and forty hours, depending on the model.

the electrodes and sends it to the brain. There it is translated into sounds.

Cochlear implants allow people with severe hearing loss to hear sounds. But like bionic eyes, they do not create a fully functional sense. Fourteen-year-old Juliet Corwin described living with cochlear implants: "Many Deaf people, and hearing people, think of cochlear implants as a 'solution' to deafness. It isn't. The technology simply helps me live with my deafness in a certain way."[6]

CHAPTER FOUR

WHAT'S NEXT FOR BIONICS IN HEALTH CARE?

The future of bionics in health care is exciting. The field is fueled by new materials and technologies. Doctors and engineers are learning more about how the human body works. With this knowledge they can create better bionic parts that improve or even save people's lives.

Research on bionics is continuing in labs around the world.

MORE NATURAL BIONIC LIMBS

Hugh Herr is a professor at the Massachusetts Institute of Technology (MIT). Herr is also a double leg amputee.

He knows firsthand how bionic limbs do not feel and act naturally. Instead, the bionic limbs feel like separate attachments. Bionic limbs receive electrical signals from the brain. These signals tell the limb how to move. However, most limbs do not send information back to the nervous system. Without feedback, a person cannot sense and feel the movement of the prosthesis. They cannot tell where and how the prosthesis is moving without looking. This one-way communication happens because nerve endings were cut during amputation.

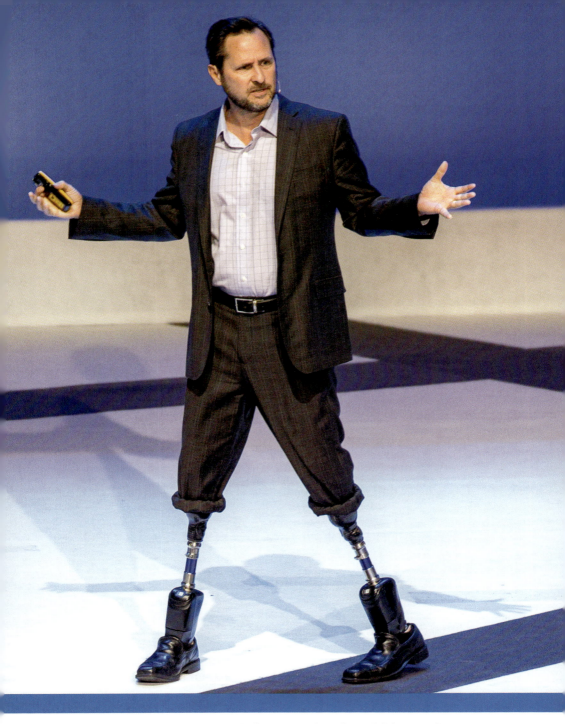

Herr has spoken at public events about his work with bionic legs.

Herr has successfully made bionic legs that feel and react like natural legs. To do this, patients must have special surgery. A surgeon links the person's nerves and muscles to the bionic leg. The nerves send information to limb muscles to make them flex and stretch as they naturally would. The sensations travel back to the spinal cord. The brain receives the information and moves the bionic limb. Herr has developed bionic ankles that mimic the real thing. Users say that their prostheses feel like actual body parts. They no longer feel and move like separate tools.

Herr's friend Jim Ewing underwent the surgery. He was fitted with one of Herr's bionic legs. He was surprised at how quickly he could use his bionic leg and foot. "I right away started using it as if it were my

BIONIC BRAIN

One day it may be possible to replace part of a brain that isn't working correctly. Scientists at the University of Southern California studied how to improve memory. They recorded the brain activity of patients while patients completed a memory task. Then they triggered the same brain activity later. In the experiment, the patients' memory skills improved. This technology could someday help people with memory problems.

own foot," Ewing recalled. "It's responding. It felt kind of like my foot had returned."[7]

BIONIC EXOSKELETONS

Disease, injuries, and strokes can cause paralysis. People affected by these things may lose the ability to walk. An exoskeleton suit can help them stand and walk again. The suit is a type of robotic frame that fits over the patient's body, legs, and feet. It helps the patient stand and supports his or her weight. A physical therapist controls the suit. The therapist can input information on the suit's computer touch screen. The computer records the patient's progress.

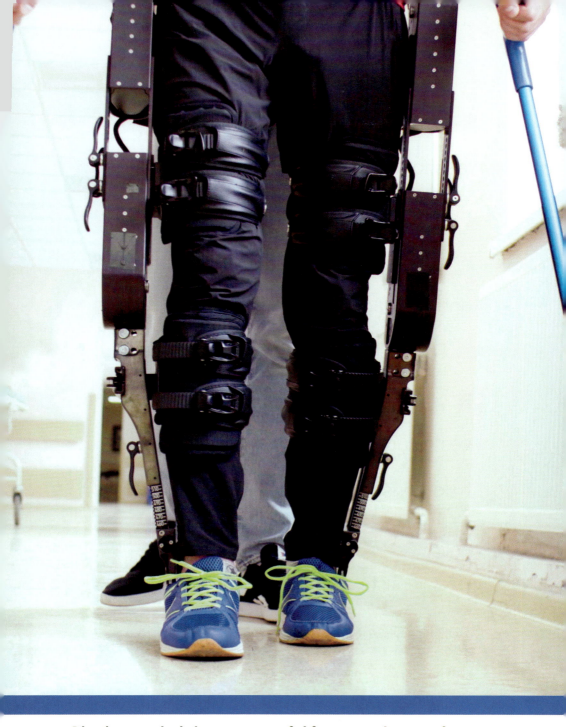

Bionic exoskeletons are useful for some types of physical therapy.

Battery-powered motors move the user's legs forward. Wearing the suit helps patients learn to balance and shift their weight. With practice, they can take steps and walk again.

Some types of exoskeletons are used to prevent workplace injuries. Exoskeleton vests support the upper body. They help construction workers lift heavy objects safely.

Scientists are also experimenting with pairing exoskeletons and brain implants. In 2019, a paralyzed man was able to control an exoskeleton suit using signals from his

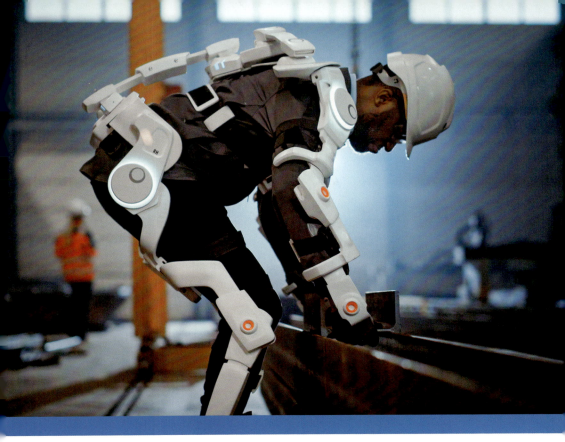

Full bionic exoskeletons could one day be used in places like factories and warehouses.

brain. It took two years to train the system

to turn his thoughts into movements.

BIONIC ORGANS

Skin is the largest organ in the human body.

It acts as a barrier that protects the body

against harm. Skin keeps in water and heat. It keeps out disease. It also provides the sense of touch. Researchers are in the beginning stages of creating electronic skin. They call it e-skin. E-skin could add the sense of touch to bionic limbs.

Flexible e-skin is made from elastic materials. It can include many useful features. "The ideal e-skin will mimic the many natural functions of human skin, such as sensing temperature and touch, accurately and in real time," says scientist Yichen Cai.[8] One goal is to apply e-skin to bionic limbs. Researchers at Stanford

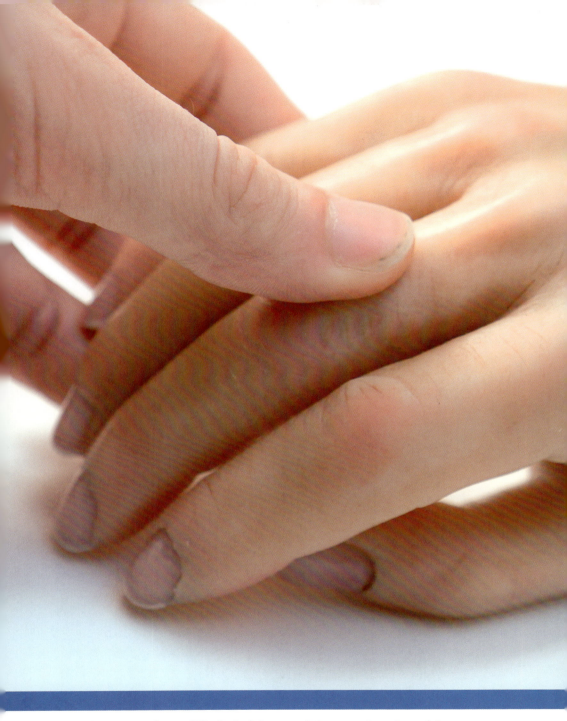

Advances in artificial skin could one day lead to more lifelike bionic limbs.

University made an e-skin so sensitive that it can detect a butterfly landing on a prosthesis. Bionic limbs covered in e-skin could help users identify the shape and texture of objects that they touch and hold.

There is a great need for other artificial organs and organ implants. There are not enough donated organs for everyone. People often wait years for an organ transplant. Many die before receiving the organ they need. Bionic organs and organ parts offer a solution.

Millions of people around the world suffer from advanced kidney disease.

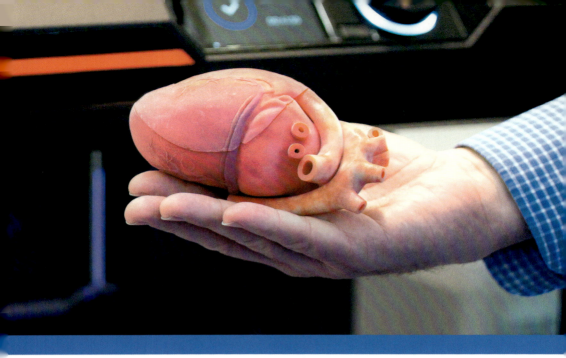

Scientists hope that in the future, they will be able to create artificial organs using 3D printers.

One of the kidneys' important jobs is to filter **toxins** from the blood. People with diseased kidneys spend several hours a week having dialysis. During this treatment, they are hooked up to a machine. The machine cleans the toxins from their blood. In the future, dialysis may not be needed.

Scientists from The Kidney Project at the University of California, San Francisco, developed an artificial kidney. The device is implanted in the body. It has filters that remove toxins from the blood. The bionic kidney eliminates the need for dialysis treatments. People will be able to lead more normal lives.

BIONIC BLOOD

Red blood cells carry oxygen around inside the body. They are flexible and can squeeze through tiny spaces. Scientists have created artificial blood cells that have the same properties. In the future, artificial blood cells may help fight cancer. They may carry anticancer drugs throughout a person's body.

IS BIONIC BETTER?

Bionic body parts were once just science fiction. But bionics are real, and the field continues to grow rapidly. There are many questions to consider about how bionics are changing the way people live. Bionic organs can help people live longer. Bionic limbs improve the quality of life for people with limb differences. There are many benefits to bionics. But there are some potential downsides as well.

One big issue is fairness. Many bionic devices cost thousands of dollars. Not everyone can afford to receive bionic

As bionics technology improves, more people than ever before will be able to use these life-changing devices.

replacements. People worry that wealthy individuals may be the only ones to benefit from bionic devices. Another issue centers on privacy. Brain implants could someday read and process thoughts. This could raise major privacy concerns. People would need control over who could read their thoughts. As the technology advances, experts in medical **ethics** are thinking about issues like these.

Today, bionic devices in health care are improving lives around the world. Exciting developments are happening at research facilities in many countries. These technologies promise to continue changing the lives of people who need them.

GLOSSARY

axon

a nerve fiber that carries nerve impulses to a muscle

cosmetic

something done or made just for appearance

ethics

a system of moral principles that guides how people make decisions

implanted

placed inside of

mimic

to copy

prosthesis

an artificial body part

residual

a part remaining after the other parts have been removed

toxins

poisonous substances

SOURCE NOTES

INTRODUCTION: A NEW ARM

1. Patrick Kane, "Being Bionic: How Technology Transformed My Life," *Guardian*, November 15, 2018. www.theguardian.com.

CHAPTER ONE: WHAT IS THE HISTORY OF BIONICS IN HEALTH CARE?

2. Quoted in "Life and Limb," *Harvard Medical School*, January 18, 2021. https://hms.harvard.edu.

CHAPTER TWO: HOW DO BIONICS IN HEALTH CARE WORK?

3. Quoted in Pam Belluck, "Device Offers Partial Vision for the Blind," *New York Times*, February 14, 2013. www.nytimes.com.

4. Quoted in Carolyn Kimmel, "From a Wooden Hand to Bionic Fingers," *Penn Live*, February 16, 2014. www.pennlive.com.

CHAPTER THREE: HOW ARE DOCTORS USING BIONICS TODAY?

5. Quoted in Paulette Campbell, "Titanium Implant Unlocks New Levels of Operability for Prosthetic Arm," *Johns Hopkins University*, January 12, 2016. https://hub.jhu.edu.

6. Juliet Corwin, "The Lonely World Between the Hearing and the Deaf," *Washington Post*, January 28, 2021. www.washingtonpost.com.

CHAPTER FOUR: WHAT'S NEXT FOR BIONICS IN HEALTH CARE?

7. Quoted in Gideon Gil, "Pioneering Surgery Makes a Prosthetic Foot Feel Like the Real Thing," *STAT*, May 30, 2018. www.statnews.com.

8. Quoted in "Electronic Skin Has Strong Future Ahead," *Tribune India*, February 3, 2021. www.tribuneindia.com.

FOR FURTHER RESEARCH

BOOKS

Holly Duhig, *Bionic Limbs*. New York: Gareth Stevens Publishing, 2018.

Leah Kaminski, *Bionic Bodies*. New York: Full Tilt Press, 2020.

Christine Zuchora-Walske, *Bionic Eyes*. Minneapolis, MN: Abdo Publishing, 2018.

INTERNET SOURCES

Jeanette Ferrara, "Bionic Beasts," *SuperScience*, September 2020. https://superscience.scholastic.com.

Bill Gates, "Bionic Arms Empower Kids to Express Themselves," *Gates Notes*, June 11, 2018. www.gatesnotes.com.

Sean R. Mills and Mark Fletcher, "Here's What Music Sounds Like Through an Auditory Implant," *The Conversation*, March 31, 2019. www.theconversation.com.

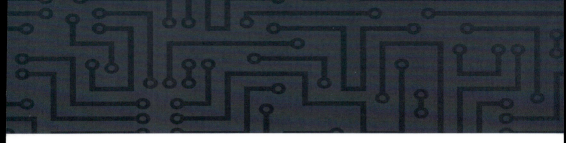

WEBSITES

Amputee Coalition
www.amputee-coalition.org

This site is dedicated to providing information on limb loss and supporting amputees and their families. Visitors to the site can learn about coping with limb loss, new prosthetic technologies, and many other subjects related to limb amputation.

Hero Arm
https://openbionics.com/hero-arm/

The official website for the Hero Arm includes information on how this bionic device works, what it can do, and how it has changed people's lives.

Medline Plus: Artificial Limbs
https://medlineplus.gov/artificiallimbs.html

This website from the US government features information about artificial limbs, including links to cutting-edge research.

INDEX

attachment to body, 31–33, 44–47

bionic ears, 51–55
bionic eyes, 48–51
blood, 69–70
bones, 25, 44–47

cochlear implants, 53–55
comfort, 6, 8, 22, 44–45
cost, 43–44, 71–72
Crandell, David, 27

dolphins, 27

electrical signals, 24, 28–29,
    33–35, 36–38, 49–50, 53, 58
exoskeletons, 62–65

Gerber, Joel, 37–38

Hero Arm, 39, 43–44
Herr, Hugh, 57–62
history of prosthetics, 14–24

Kane, Patrick, 12–13

Matheny, Johnny, 47–48
medical ethics, 71–73
myoelectric prosthetics, 24, 36–38

organs, 44, 65–70, 71

Paré, Ambroise, 18–20
phantom limb syndrome (PLS), 35
prosthetic arms, 6–10, 18, 30,
    36–37, 39, 43–44, 47
prosthetic hands, 8, 18–20, 31,
    37–39
prosthetic legs, 10, 13, 16, 18, 22,
    30, 45, 60–61

retinal implants, 48–51

skin, 65–68

3D printing, 41–44

wars, 21–22

IMAGE CREDITS

Cover: © photographer/iStockphoto
5: © Dmitry Markov152/
Shutterstock Images
7: © SolStock/iStockphoto
9: © 22Images Studio/
Shutterstock Images
11: © SeventyFour/
Shutterstock Images
12: © Gorodenkoff/
Shutterstock Images
15: © Skoda/Shutterstock Images
17: © Science Museum, London/
Wellcome Collection
19: Wellcome Collection
21: © Science & Society Picture
Library/Getty Images
23: © A. Garratt/Wellcome Collection
26: © Gorodenkoff/
Shutterstock Images
29: © whitehoune/Shutterstock Images
31: © Katy Pack/Shutterstock Images
34: © onurdongel/iStockphoto
37: © Medicimage/Science Source
38: © yurakrasil/Shutterstock Images

41: © stockddvideo/
Shutterstock Images
43: © Djordje Novakov/
Shutterstock Images
46: © Olena Yakobchuk/
Shutterstock Images
49: © DutchScenery/iStockphoto
51: © Philippe Psaila/Science Source
52: © Sladic/iStockphoto
54: © Ivan_Shenets/
Shutterstock Images
57: © Zoriana Zaitseva/
Shutterstock Images
59: © Robert Marquardt/Getty Images
Entertainment/Getty Images
63: © Ivan Chudakov/
Shutterstock Images
65: © Gorodenkoff/
Shutterstock Images
67: © Lara Joy/Shutterstock Images
69: © Scharfsinn/Shutterstock Images
72: © Olena Yakobchuk/
Shutterstock Images

ABOUT THE AUTHOR

Cecilia Pinto McCarthy has written more than forty nonfiction books for young readers. When she is not writing, she teaches classes at a nature center. She lives north of Boston, Massachusetts, with her family.